CW01647517

Prayers for Peace and Friendship

Prayer, readings and reflections to change the world

Gaynor Cobb

kevin mayhew

First Published in 2022 by Kevin Mayhew Ltd,
Fengate Farm,
Rattlesden,
Bury St Edmunds,
Suffolk, IP30 0SZ

ISBN (paperback): 9781838581459
ISBN (eBook): 9781838581466
Paperback product code: 1501718
eBook product code: 1501719

To ChildAid Eastern Europe for their support of vulnerable children, young people and their families and for the healing and reconstruction of Ukraine. May God grant all those suffering in war torn regions, a lasting peace.

For you shall go out in joy,
and be led back in peace;
the mountains and the hills
before you
shall burst into song,
and all the trees of the field shall clap
their hands.
(Isaiah 55:12)

Contents

Introduction

United Nations Sustainable Development Goal 16 is peace, justice and strong institutions.

It is represented by a dove holding an olive branch on a gavel of justice.

This is a most important goal for our world, because without peace, we are unable to achieve any of our other goals.

Go therefore and make disciples of all nations,
baptizing them in the name of the Father and of the Son
and of the Holy Spirit,
and teaching them to obey everything that I have commanded you.
And remember, I am with you always, to the end of the age.
(Matthew 28:19-20)

Jesus told his disciples to go out into the world to baptise people of every country and to teach them about God's kingdom. The Prince of Peace was sending his followers out to deliver his message of brotherhood; the message of Christianity, to tell them about the two greatest commandments, that they should love God and love each other as they loved themselves.

This is certainly a message of peace and it is to be given to all nations. It is a worldwide message of love.

Jesus assures them that he will be with them at all times.

Prayer is powerful. Let us use it to make a difference in our world.

We know that Jesus tells us in Matthew's Gospel that when two or three are gathered in his name, he is there. Many of us have personal experiences that demonstrate the power of our prayers to God. It may be that someone was ill, or experiencing difficult times. We do feel that God hears our prayers and there is a great power of prayer when people gather together.

On one occasion, I took part in a remote prayer exercise, where people joined together at a particular time wherever they were. The prayers were given to help a desperate world situation. Within a few days of our prayer, aid had reached people very much in need. It was a breakthrough.

When we pray, we may form pictures in our minds. This visualisation can also be powerful.

It may be beautiful flowers or countryside if we are giving thanks to God for his creation.

This gives an impression of peacefulness that matches our prayers.

Light is an especially powerful force of thought. This is particularly true of the cross of light.

The cross on which Christ defeated death shines with a special power that moves us and cuts through the darkness of pain and despair. As a way to bring peace, the cross of light gives us a Christian visualisation that is unmatched.

In recent times, our world has been very much in need of prayer for peace and many of us have been gathering together to send our prayers to God and our hopes for a peaceful resolution of conflict.

So many people are in need of healing prayer because they live in fear, pain or loss.

Often, we feel powerless to solve these problems. Whatever we are able to do, our prayers can be offered to God and we can be sure that they are heard and will make a difference.

Mother Teresa said:

'I used to believe that prayer changes things, but now I know that prayer changes us, and we change things.'

I agree that we change as we offer our prayers to God and we become more committed to particular causes and actions but I also believe that as God hears our prayers, prayer does have the power to change the world.

I hope that the prayers and Bible verses in this book will be helpful as you offer your own prayers for peace.

Chapter 1

Finding Our Own Peace

The Lord is my shepherd, I shall not want.
He makes me lie down in green pastures;
he leads me beside still waters;
he restores my soul.
He leads me in right paths
for his name's sake.
(Psalm 23. 1-3)

Reflection

The well-known psalm paints a picture of a life of peace because we are in God's hands.

It is as if we are led into the peace of the countryside where we find calming water.

Here our troubled souls are restored with rest and we are able to make the decision to follow the Lord our

God and thus to return to the right path if we have wandered away.

In this way, we are like lost sheep and God is the shepherd.

In Ezekiel 34:31, God calls us the sheep of his pasture. He has made a covenant of peace to protect his people.

Jesus says he is the Good Shepherd in the Gospel of St. John and he keeps the gate by which those who are saved enter heaven. He helps us to find our own peace.

As Christians, we can find our own peace through prayer, the words of the Bible and silent meditation.

To think about

Where do you find your own peace?

Prayer

Loving Father,
Thank you for bringing us peace,
even when our souls are troubled with the worries of daily life.
You help us to understand that we can set problems aside, coming to you, laying down our burdens.
May we always seek you in the silence, taking time from busy days.
Finding you in prayer gives calming, healing peace.
Nothing is too small to bring before you.
Each troubling thought shared to be
cast away.
We find you in the beauty of the countryside,
in stillness, or even in the fresh breeze in our hair.
Wandering beside flowing streams, our spirits are restored.
In the noise of the city, you are there.
When sound and sights assail our senses,
still we can find you if we search within.
Reaching deep inside, a silent, whispered soul-felt prayer
finds your calm soothing presence.
Help us to reach for your guiding hand,
bringing peace wherever we are.
Thus we are able to serve you by serving others,
knowing that, safe within your love,
we have found our own peace.
Amen.

Chapter 2

The Peace of Nature

How beautiful upon the mountains
are the feet of the messenger who
announces peace,
who brings good news,
who announces salvation,
who says to Zion, 'Your God reigns.'
(Isaiah 52:7)

Reflection

Here we have the image of a messenger walking the hills to bring news of peace from God.

The picture of mountains in our mind's eye is of a peaceful vista we can see for miles around. The hills themselves bring a soothing calm and all is well with the world because we love God and he is our King.

Perhaps there has been conflict but now peace is announced and we can drink in the view and the peace of nature around us.

The messenger may be nature itself, because it is often through nature that we are able to connect to God and to experience peace.

Mountains are uplifting, giving the impression of majesty and also bringing us nearer to God.

Jesus often climbed a mountain in order to be closer to his Father.

This also helps us to understand how we are uplifted when we pray to God.

Perhaps the most accurate interpretation, is that Jesus himself is the beautiful messenger. He announces peace, good news and through him we have salvation.

He tells us about God's kingdom and brings us to the Father who reigns over us as we look up to the mountain top.

To think about

Do you have a special place of natural beauty where your spirits are uplifted?

Prayer

Creator God,
We gaze upon the hills to seek your peace.
As we walk, we feel closer to you, as time stands still.
We give thanks for the gift of your wonderful creation:
the majestic mountains, the sound of flowing rivers
and the peace and shade of trees.
All nature feeds our souls with your love.

Help us to seek you in prayer in difficult times,
to find upliftment within.
When our hearts are troubled,
it is to nature that we turn for calm and healing.
We pray that all people will find you
in the beauty of the world
you have made for us.
We give thanks for your son, our Saviour,
the beautiful messenger
who brings the truth of your kingdom.
Through him we come to you,
receiving your grace
and the peace of your forgiveness.
May all be free to seek your peace
and to receive this your messenger,
Jesus Christ,
our guide to eternal life.
Amen.

Chapter 3

Friendship

But Ruth said,
Do not press me to leave you
or to turn back from following you!
Where you go, I will go;
where you lodge, I will lodge;
your people shall be my people,
and your God my God.
Where you die, I will die-
there will I be buried.
(Ruth 1: 16-17)

Reflection

The friendship of Ruth and Naomi is one of the great stories of the Bible.

Naomi's husband and sons had died while they were living in Moab and she was left with her two daughters-in- law, who were Moabite women.

Naomi returned to her land of Judah but tried to persuade her daughters- in- law to return to their own mother's house. Although Orpah did this reluctantly, Ruth would not agree to leave Naomi. She spoke the beautiful words quoted in the book of Ruth 1: 16-17.

The passage describes a closeness that provides comfort in adversity and a true commitment.

Ruth turned to worship of the Living God when she went to Judah.

The story ends happily because Ruth married Boaz who was related to Naomi and they cared for one another.

Ruth is known as a kind friend and her son Obed was the grandfather of David.

To think about

We often lose contact with people over time. Is there a friend you could contact again?

Prayer

Loving Father,
We give you thanks for the gift of friendship.
Jesus chose disciples who supported him as friends throughout his ministry and beyond his death.
He taught the priceless value of true friendship and the need to travel the journey of life with the companionship of others.
John Donne wrote, 'no man is an island' and we know that this is true indeed.
We thank you for friends we can turn to, sharing our worries, because a listening ear soothes and puts things in perspective.
At difficult times,
We give thanks for the support of friends.
How grateful we are that we can share moments of happiness with others.
Memories are made to be cherished across the years, enjoyed over again in quiet moments.
When we hear laughter, everyday matters can be laid aside for a little.
We can return to normality, refreshed with a new optimism and able to face each small challenge with renewed energy.
We thank you for the chance to share our lives with others through friendship.
Amen

Chapter 4

International Friendship

For as in one body we have many members,
and not all the members
have the same function,
so we, who are many,
are one body in Christ,
and individually
we are members one of another.
(Romans 12: 4-5)

Reflection

Paul's letter to the church in Rome explains how Christians will receive new life in Christ.

He tells them that although they are all different, they each have a function, a special role to play and that together, they form the body of Christ: The Church. As they bring their gifts to Christ and his church on earth, they will combine to form one special body of God's church.

We reach out in friendship to individuals but we can also find friendship between countries if

governments pursue this. Soft diplomacy extends influence through culture and education, rather than the hard power of politics or economics. The soft diplomacy of cultural, sporting and educational links can help to develop understanding between nations. Through this understanding, we hope that lasting peace can be achieved because countries maintain positive contact.

As a world, states are individual and yet they are also different. It is in celebrating differences and the aspects that make countries special, that creates the world we live in. As nations form international friendship links, they exchange ideas as well as cultural experiences.

Peace is maintained and nurtured by valuing the talents and contribution that all nations bring to our global village. This is to enrich the world and not to exploit individual states.

The commitment to peace through the friendship of all nations, depends on

education and opportunities for the people of all countries. Where people are not able to access employment opportunities through lack of education, their state cannot come to the world table as a friendship partner very easily.

World organisations, such as the United Nations must ensure that richer nations do not exploit poorer ones. Friendship links should be just that and not the means to acquire material wealth or other advantages.

Paul goes on to say that love should be genuine, with mutual affection and that Christians should try to outdo each other in showing honour.

He also advises them to persevere in prayer.

To think about

Do you think that the soft diplomacy of friendship links between nations is important?

Prayer

Loving Father,
We praise you for all our blessings,
received through our lives as one body in Christ.
Help us to use our gifts in your service,
holding fast to what is good.
We pray for all nations.
Guide them as they reach out to one another.
May they celebrate all that brings them close
and also everything that makes them different.
We pray for special links of international friendship,
to enrich our world with every colour, sound and word.
Help all nations to draw closer through education and culture.
May these connections give opportunities to all people,
especially to those most in need.
As we praise you Father, help us to value what is good
and to stand strong against those who turn from truth and justice.
May the world know and use its strength against any oppressor,
so that peace can be maintained.
We know that we are stronger if we stand together.
We pray that all will stand firmly against those who deny their people rights and justice.
We pray for international friendship,
For the greater good.
Amen.

Chapter 5

Forgiveness

**Then Peter came and said to him,
'Lord, if another member of the church
sins against me, how often should I forgive?
As many as seven times?'
Jesus said to him,
'Not seven times, but I tell you,
seventy-seven times.'
(Matthew 18:21-22)**

Reflection

When we think of forgiveness, this is the only passage we need from the Bible.

It tells us that there is no limit to the times we must forgive others.

After this reply to Peter, Jesus went on to tell the parable of the unforgiving servant.

The slave who was pardoned by his master over a debt, failed to show mercy to the other slave who owed him money. He had the debtor thrown into prison.

As he had not been able to forgive, he himself was not forgiven but was handed over to be tortured.

The moral of the story is, if you expect forgiveness, show mercy yourself. If we forgive others, God will forgive us.

Sometimes it is difficult to forgive and yet we know that it happens even when terrible events have taken place.

We are also aware that God has to forgive us far more than we ever forgive anyone else.

We fail him so many times and rely upon his forgiveness and absolution. We receive this because of the sacrifice of his Son, our Saviour.

To think about

Is it always possible to forgive?

Prayer

Loving Father,
As we follow the words of Jesus to Peter,
help us to forgive others as many times as we need to.
May we be quick to heal wounds and division.
May we be slow to find fault with those around us
and reluctant to judge other people.
Guide us to the realisation that we are all alike.
We all fail and falter.
Through empathy and compassion, may we have the ability to
understand and forgive those who fail us.
Father, help us to forgive ourselves.
In this way we can try to be closer to your Son.
Following him, we are renewed in your love
because his death brought us your grace for forgiveness.
As sinners, we come before you, trusting in your forgiveness and mercy.
At your table, as we share his body and blood,
may we be filled with your Holy Spirit,
to go into our imperfect world,
as disciples of the Saviour,
cleansed and ready to do your will.
Amen.

Chapter 6

The Peace of Christ

Peace I leave with you; my peace I give to you. I do not give to you as the world gives.
Do not let your hearts be troubled, and do not let them be afraid.
(John 14:27)

Reflection

This is a very important assurance from Lord Jesus to his disciples.

He knew what was going to happen to him but could not tell them about it in detail. The words given would come back to his friends over and over again after his death.

Jesus was telling them that he was going to his Father in heaven and that he would be blessed to be there. He knew that they would be full of sorrow because they would not be able to speak with him as they had while he was on earth. The disciples would face a time of great fear and uncertainty and he wanted them to know that there was nothing to fear in the future.

Jesus says that he does not give as the world does. He does not give riches on earth but they have found peace through being his special followers.

Whatever happens on earth, Jesus has promised heavenly peace which is of greater value than anything material and this will transcend all fear and doubt.

The disciples would find their strength on earth and in heaven through the peace

of Christ.

As Christians, we know that whatever life has in store for us, we have been promised the peace of Christ when we die. This links with the promise of eternal life, given through baptism, confirmation and communion.

We are blessed because we believe and this gives us the peace of Christ.

There is a deep sense of peace which comes from knowing Jesus.

It is eternal peace, but it seems unlikely that anyone could achieve peace in heaven if they remain in conflict with others on the earth. Once again, we are reminded of the importance of healing and forgiveness.

As Christians, we are all disciples of Jesus.

Sometimes we may feel that being Christian can be uncomfortable because we have to make demands on ourselves. The peace of Christ is there and our faith helps us to feel this. There are many occasions during worship when it appears close to us, especially during times of prayer and meditation.

To think about

Take a moment to think about the way that you receive the peace of Christ.

Prayer

Eternal Father,
We thank you for the peace that Lord Jesus has given us.
We know that even conflict on earth cannot take away the peace of eternal life, given through your Son.
When fear is all around us and life seems so uncertain, it is easy to be in despair, without hope for the future.
Our faith remains strong, even at these times because of the promise of the Saviour.
The peace of Christ remains with us and with all those who struggle in war torn countries.
We pray for the ability to forgive and by so doing, to feel strong in the peace granted by our Saviour to all believers.
May we be filled with the Holy Spirit as we work and pray for peace on earth.
We pray for your church in the world.
May it be strong to stand against violence and oppression,
wherever it is found.
May it give hope and support to all in fear and need.
May it be for them the light of Christ, leading them to his peace,
whatever they face in their daily lives.
Amen.

Chapter 7

United Nations

He shall judge between the nations,
and shall arbitrate for many peoples;
they shall beat their swords into ploughshares,
and their spears into pruning-hooks;
nation shall not lift up sword against nation,
neither shall they learn war any more.
(Isaiah 2:4)

Reflection

The United Nations Sustainable Development Goal 16 is peace, justice and strong institutions.

Isaiah gives us the hope that war will be banished because God will judge those who bring conflict. Farming will take the place of fighting so that even weapons will become farming implements.

This wonderful ideal represents the essence of the United Nations, where all countries can stand together, removing the need for individual blame.

In December 1959, the USSR presented a statue to the United Nations, based on this verse from Isaiah. We may well think about these words in the light of the events of 2022.

Many people in the world need food to prevent starvation and wars cause the displacement of people which exacerbates the struggle for survival.

Peace is vital, so that the world can turn its attention to the challenge of feeding its people and providing for their basic needs.

As a world we must stand for justice and institutions that are strong enough to stand against tyranny and oppression.

A powerful United Nations offers the possibility of peaceful solutions to conflict

among nation states.

To think about

Take time to visit www.un.org the website of the United Nations.

Prayer

Eternal Father,
We pray for the United Nations,
may they have influence amongst all countries of the world.
May the peacemakers of all nations come together
to bring an end to conflict and oppression.
Let there be a desire to speak and to listen to others,
so that an understanding may be reached,
even when there is opposition from all sides.
Help all nations to heed words of wisdom,
brought about through meeting and discussion.
Help mediation to be strong where it is needed,
in order to bring enemies together.
We pray for a strong stand
against violence, injustice and inequality,
so that we may build a world fair for all.
May the oppressors fear the condemnation of the world,
finding nowhere to turn for support.
We pray for education,
for young people to learn
the diplomacy that will help to solve the struggles of future years.
We pray that,
standing together for freedom,
the United Nations will bring your love
and righteousness to all.
Amen.

Chapter 8

Paths to War and Peace

Then Jesus said to him,
'Put your sword back into its place; for all who take the sword will perish by the sword.'
(Matthew 26: 52)

Reflection

Jesus gives a warning to those who cause violence on earth.

It can only bring harm to you if you live in this way.

Matthew tells us that the words were spoken when Jesus was arrested and one of those with him drew his sword and cut off the ear of the slave of the high priest. Jesus knew that the arrest had to take place and would not let his followers fight. This was a particular situation.

Jesus is saying that God is never on your side if you wage war. This surely means those who cause conflict because of their own demands.

Sometimes, it has been necessary to defend freedom and civilisation by fighting an aggressor.

This is a different situation because there are times that we can bring about a peaceful situation and improve civilisation by fighting oppression.

In his letter to the twelve tribes, James writes of conflicts and disputes which come from cravings.

Wars often come from greed for power and land. James says that God opposes the proud but gives grace to those who are humble. Humility is a path to peace.

It may be that war will give short term gains but God can see the bigger picture and we can believe that those who make war cannot prosper in the long term.

To think about

Can it ever be right to wage war?

Prayer

Eternal Father,
We know that greed leads to war.
As nations rise up against nations
for power, land and influence,
we know that you are never on their side.
We pray that humankind
will learn to deal with conflicts
and the desires that drive them.
May mediation be at the forefront
of relations between states.
Father, guide them to turn to
diplomacy and mediation
before they turn to war and aggression.
Help them to seek the common ground between them
to preserve the safety and security
of all people.
May paths that seem to lead to war turn away,
so that they become
pathways towards
a lasting peace
for all nations.
Amen.

Chapter 9

Countries at War

I have said this to you, so that in me you may have peace.
In the world you face persecution.
But take courage; I have conquered the world!'
(John 16:33)

Reflection

Jesus was speaking to his disciples before the events leading to his death, explaining about the events that were to come. He is really giving his friends words to recall when they are isolated and alone in fear and confusion. These words are important. They would carry his friends through the challenging times ahead.

Jesus is explaining that it is only through him that they will find peace because he has been able to rise above worldly concerns. He tells them not to fear the world of man because through him they will have the peace of eternal life. He has already defeated the world itself.

They should know that whatever happens, it is something he can overcome because the world cannot make him afraid. Jesus tells them about the great joy to come and this will take away the pain they have suffered.

After speaking to his disciples, Lord Jesus prayed to the Father to protect the friends who were given to him by God to complete his earthly mission.

The message to all of us is that the world itself cannot harm us because Jesus has defeated evil and death.

We feel that all countries in conflict believe that God is on their side and yet we recognise that this cannot be so.

We think that we can judge the right and wrong of many situations.

Countries must come to the table to talk in order to achieve a peaceful solution to their differences.

To think about

How can God be on every side? How can we mediate in difficult circumstances?

Prayer

Eternal Father,
We pray for all people who suffer
as a result of conflict between nations.
May they gain strength when they feel helpless
because of decisions made around them.
Like reeds bending in the wind,
their lives are driven this way and that.
We pray for their peace, the peace of Christ Jesus.
That, as they seek him, they will find a refuge,
calming fears and bringing hope.
We pray that the leaders of all nations in conflict
will find the will to seek the common ground that leads to peace.
May the spirit of reconciliation prevail within them,
so that solutions can be found,
even when hope seems far away.
Be with them Father when pain and anger are uppermost,
blocking all thought of mediation.
Help them to find a way through hurt and despair
towards the light of healing words
and a real pathway of peace.
We ask this in the name of Jesus Christ, our Saviour,
the Prince of Peace.
Amen.

Chapter 10

Consequences of War

The wicked are overthrown and are no more,
but the house of the righteous will stand.
(Proverbs 12: 7)

The evil are ensnared by the transgression of their lips,
but the righteous escape from trouble.
(Proverbs 12:13)

Reflection

Proverbs warns of the consequences of evildoing. It talks of lies and schemes which can only lead to destruction. It holds out the promise that the good will triumph because they have heeded the word of God and stand for truth.

Those who walk in darkness will perish and the good will walk in the light towards a brighter and brighter dawn.

This is important when evil seems to prosper in the world. We see and hear of so much that is corrupt and the strength of warfare and violence can sweep away the old, young and weak.

Sometimes ignorance survives and power comes from the barrel of a gun, rather than through education, reason and caring.

The words of Proverbs are a comfort to us when we feel despair as we look around at some places in the world.

War blights the lives of so many people and communities struggle to develop as they should because they are constantly under attack.

We can be encouraged and keep trying to right wrongs and to stand up to injustice wherever we find it, if we hold to the belief that right will prevail.

To think about

Find out about support for educational opportunities in the world today.

Prayer

Loving Father,
We pray for all those who stand against war and violence.
Give strength to all peaceful communities
as they hold onto daily life
even when they are surrounded by conflict and disruption.
May they drive out fear and ignorance,
so that education can take root,
building a stronger, peaceful future for all.
We pray that the lies of those who spread dissent and pain
will not take hold among the poor.
We pray for those who heal the wounds of war,
repairing broken lives and bringing people
together in reconciliation.
Help them to rebuild in brotherhood and truth,
finding a way forward without fear. May they stand for
the truth of our Saviour Jesus Christ,
following his word
and finding his peace.
Amen

Chapter 11

The Children of War

Blessed are the peacemakers, for they will be called children of God.
(Matthew 5:9 from The Beatitudes)

Reflection

In this famous teaching of Jesus concerning blessings, he spoke of the peacemakers as God's children, giving them a special place in heaven.

Peacemakers hold an important place in the Bible because of this verse from the Beatitudes.

Children themselves are casualties of war in many ways. They may lose parents and necessary support, their homes and education are often disrupted and they may have to leave the communities where they have grown up. Families and friendships are disrupted and lives are hurt before they have really begun.

Child soldiers are a reality of war in many countries, fighting, carrying messages and becoming involved in the trauma of conflict in ways that make them old before their time.

Even at the end of war, they are often not accepted back in their communities.

They are changed and damaged.

Girls may have their own children as a result of war violence and this starts a terrible situation for children once again.

Communities are not sure about the feelings of these children and do not know how to help them.

Despite everything, children are our hope for the future. With education and support, they can drive the changes needed in society and learn from the past. They can become blessed peacemakers themselves.

Children of war give us one of the strongest reasons to pray and work for peace.

To think about

How many countries use child soldiers?

Prayer

Loving Father,
We pray for all the children of war-torn places in the world.
May they find the light of your love, leading them out of fear and despair.
Help them to find inner strength and resilience,
so that they are able to strive for peace
and grow in wisdom.
Be with them at times of hardship and confusion.
Help them to find a guiding hand.
May we protect children of conflict and bring them to a safe haven.
We pray for the authority and power of the United Nations as they seek to prevent the use of child soldiers.
May all nations support this aim.
We pray for divided communities where there is conflict.
Father, heal the wounds when peace returns,
so that children receive the help they need to grow in love once again.
Be with all those who have lost their childhood to war.
Comfort them and help them to find a way forward,
stronger because they know you are with them.
May the seeds of peace grow within communities.
May they hold out loving arms of mercy to all children who have suffered because of war.
Amen.

Chapter 12

Peace within Countries

The effect of righteousness will be peace,
and the result of righteousness,
quietness and trust for ever.
My people will abide in a peaceful habitation,
in secure dwellings, and in quiet resting-places.
(Isaiah 32: 17-18)

Reflection

Isaiah 32 talks of the change taking place when justice prevails and a ruler is wise. People will be able to see and hear the sense given to them and they will have good judgement.

The result of these changes will be peace, quietness and trust for ever. Homes will be safe and quiet will prevail.

This is a beautiful promise that when there is a benevolent ruler or government, all is well. In biblical times, it was likely to be a ruler. Today, it is more likely to be a government. It suggests that democracy is one way to achieve peace. In righteousness, the government of the people provides peace and the people themselves also make a commitment to peace in the service of the realm.

We like to encourage service to the nation and this is often shown in the hymns we sing at special times.

The words of I Vow to Thee My Country, were written by Sir Cecil Spring-Rice (1859-1918) and set to music by Gustav Holst.

The hymn speaks of the service of love to a country on earth, but it also tells of the heavenly realm which has ways of gentleness and paths of peace.

When civil war arises, it is hard to imagine that anyone gains. Even if there is a peaceful outcome to internal conflict, the resulting situation often creates weaker government and suffering for the people. Such conflicts often appear to be mere power struggles that fail to help anyone.

To think about

Is freedom of speech important in order to preserve democracy?

Prayer

Eternal Father,
We pray for righteousness in all government.
May people be empowered in freedom
to stand for justice and democracy.
We pray for a world where the people of all nations
can live in security and peace,
without fear from factions within countries or from outside.
We know that there are many places
where governments are unstable and changes take place.
The people suffer and are not able to live peaceful lives with their families.
We pray that people will learn to live together and to heal divisions.
Where there is separation, may there be unity and cooperation.
We think of the heavenly kingdom and the life to come
and we give thanks for gentleness and quiet resting places.
Our souls restored, you lead us along the right paths
and we do not fear evil because you are with us.
We think of your goodness and mercy
and the promise
that we shall dwell in your house for evermore.
Father help us to strive to create heaven on earth.
Guide us as we work for all your children.
Amen.

Chapter 13

Praying for Particular Situations

He said, 'Do not fear, greatly beloved, you are safe.
Be strong and courageous!'
When he spoke to me, I was strengthened and said,
'Let my lord speak, for you have strengthened me.'
(Daniel 10:19)

Reflection

Daniel had visions, showing battles between kings of the world. These led to the end of time.

They were interpreted as a time when the righteous would be saved and be led to glory.

The Bible tells us of many battles, especially in the Old Testament. Perhaps this underlines the fact that human nature has not changed and we still struggle to overcome many of the same things. The desire for power, control and territory remains and we work to improve our world situation.

There are ongoing situations in a number of countries that are a particular cause for concern.

In our intercessions, we remember them because we believe in the power of prayer.

When we are gathered together we are able to feel moved by the strength of our prayer and worship.

Sitting alone, we can also think and pray for the countries where there is so much suffering.

If we visualise a cross of light with its beams shining into the area of conflict, this may help our prayers by providing a focus of thought.

Prayers for Ukraine, the Holy Land and Middle East, Afghanistan and countries in Africa follow.

Chapter 14

Ukraine

Eternal Father,

We pray for the people of Ukraine.

Be with them at this time of fear and conflict

as they face an unknown future.

May they feel the love and support of a caring world,

even as they try to understand this terrible situation.

We pray that the light of hope will enter the darkness of despair.

May strength be given to those who seek to bring peace and healing.

Guide those who need to leave the danger.

May they find safety and the help they need.

As strangers reach out to strangers,

may the spark of your love burn more brightly,

to show the world that good will triumph over evil.

We pray for the people of Russia.

Help them to know the truth.

Support them in this time of confusion,

when evil actions from within have turned the world against them.

May they overcome the darkness of dictatorship,

to find a future of brotherhood and friendship.

We pray for the young men who find themselves

fighting those they feel close to.

Father, be with them all.

May violence turn to healing.

Help world leaders to stand together

against this oppression.

Guide them to make a difference.

We pray for peace.

May understanding enter the minds of those who plan for war.

Help them to know that there is no future through this conflict.

May the futility of war become clear to them.

We pray that the road to peace is the only way ahead,

No matter how hard to take,

may this be the only road possible.

Amen.

Chapter 15

The Holy Land and The Middle East

Heavenly Father,

We pray for peace in this troubled land,

where your Son, our Saviour walked long ago.

Its people have been special to you for many years past.

You have guided them with Moses,

out of the wilderness

and here into the promised land.

May all of Abraham's children live in harmony together.

May they recognise the message of love

brought to the world by Lord Jesus,

the Prince of Peace.

May those in authority

seek to meet

in the spirit of friendship and reconciliation.

May all understand the true meaning of brotherhood

and find the road to a lasting peace.

We pray that they will follow the light of Christ

to bring love, serenity

and the sunshine of the spirit

to this beautiful and sacred place.

In the name of Christ,

Amen.

Chapter 16

Afghanistan

Eternal Father,

We pray for the people of Afghanistan.

May they live peaceful lives without the threat

of violence.

We pray for the women and girls of Afghanistan.

May they be given the right of education

and the freedom to live lives of fulfilment.

We pray that the men of the Taliban

may find enlightenment as they seek to know you.

We know that repression cannot bring peace: only pain.

We pray for understanding

and acceptance of human rights.

May all the people of Afghanistan

find peace and freedom once again,

without repression caused by ignorance.

Father, we know that without education,

people can live in fear of progress.

Change can be difficult for those who do not know

how to cope with the modern world.

Help them to rise above their own ignorance

to seek peace and understanding.

We pray for freedom once again,

bringing light in the darkness.

Amen.

Chapter 17

Africa

Eternal Father,

We pray for the continent of Africa.

For its many countries and people.

There are so many challenges as Africa is rising.

Its children are growing and there are many young people.

May their energy and creativity

help to drive the progress that is needed

so that all African nations can prosper

and live in peace with one another.

We pray for lasting peace in Sudan,

Central African Republic, Ethiopia, Somalia, Nigeria and Mozambique.

We pray for educational opportunities to be given to all children:

boys and girls.

Protect schools from the harm caused by ignorance and fear of progress.

We pray for the environment.

Help those who work with innovation to solve the problems caused by climate change.

May wealthier countries give their support to Africa

so that a real difference can be made to the lives of the poor.

We pray for democracy in all African nations,

working for peace and driving out corruption.

Father, we know that through peace,

progress can be achieved.

We pray for hope for the future

in the name of your Son,

our Saviour, Jesus Christ.

Amen.

Chapter 18

For Human Rights

He has told you, O mortal, what
is good;
and what does the Lord require of you but to do
justice, and to love kindness,
and to walk humbly with
your God?
(Micah 6:8)

Reflection

This verse inspires a prayer of penitence that may be used before Holy Communion, when we ask God to direct what we shall be. It is linked to the two greatest commandments because we cannot love God and our neighbour if we are not just, merciful and humble.

Treating all people with kindness and with justice before the law gives human rights of dignity and equality. Acting with humility also suggests these attributes.

We are told in Micah that God requires justice and mercy and that, corruption, cheating and violence will be punished. The Almighty clearly desires people to be treated fairly, so that their human rights should be respected.

The prayer of penitence shows us that we must work hard to deliver human rights to everyone, because that is the standard God requires. We ask him to help us to amend what we are if we are failing him in any way.

There are still crimes against humanity and many people suffer the oppression of their human rights every day. We know that there is much to do and that our prayers are needed to right these wrongs.

To think about

Have we done enough to improve human rights for all?

Prayer

Eternal Father,
We pray for all the people of the world.
May we strive to uphold human rights,
so that all people are treated with respect and dignity,
being equal before the law in all nations.
Father, as we walk with you,
we know that we must be kind, just and merciful,
showing love for our neighbour and caring for one another.
We pray that our world will grow in love for humanity.
Protect those who are threatened by criminal gangs
and give strength to law enforcement to provide safety.
May we fight fear that preys upon poverty and oppression.
We know that the poor should have as many rights as the rich and yet this is not always true.
Give power to the United Nations,
so that all countries are held to account
for their actions and treatment of citizens.
We pray for all political prisoners,
those whose freedom has been taken from them
because they have spoken out in opposition to a government.
May we fight to uphold democracy,
so that all nations grant free speech
and free and fair elections are held in all countries.
We ask this in the name of our Saviour, Jesus Christ.
Amen.

Chapter 19

The Displaced

Now after they had left, an angel of the Lord appeared to Joseph in a dream and said, 'Get up, take the child and his mother, and flee to Egypt, and remain there until I tell you; for Herod is about to search for the child, to destroy him.' (Matthew 2:13)

Reflection

Joseph, Mary and Jesus were displaced people because of the threat from Herod.

The Wise Men had been asked by Herod to inform him of the whereabouts of the child, because he said he wanted to worship Jesus, but actually he wished to kill him as a dynastic rival for power. Both the kings and

Joseph had warning dreams and Herod was unsuccessful in his plan.

When Herod died, another dream advised Joseph to move back to Israel from Egypt and he returned to Nazareth where Jesus was able to have a peaceful childhood.

Although Jesus was not threatened by war, he can still be regarded as a refugee. The danger from Herod was very real and infants were killed by Herod's orders at the time, as he tried to find Jesus. It is interesting that Egypt, which had enslaved the children of Israel, gave safety to the Messiah.

Refugees hold a special place in the hearts of Christians because they know that Jesus was himself a refugee.

War drives people from their homes and causes great movements of people, so that the world becomes a global village. Some people are able to settle in different countries, finding safety and security, but others return home as soon as they are able to. Despite the power of cultural and national ties, safety and the ability to find employment are the most important factors in determining where people decide to live.

Uncontrolled population movements are certainly a global problem, especially for those involved. Children in particular suffer and education is disrupted. Deaths occur, especially as a result of criminal people trafficking. One could argue that for the traffickers, war and persecution are an important part of their business.

To think about?

How can the world solve the problem of displaced people?

Prayer

Eternal Father,
We pray for all those who are displaced by war.
Guide and help them as they travel in search of safety and a new life.
We remember that Jesus was a refugee for a time
and give thanks that he and his parents found a home in Egypt
until danger had passed.
Father, we pray for an end to people trafficking.
We know that lives are lost and that money gained fuels criminal activity
which produces more misery.
Give strength to those working to combat this evil trade in despair.
Bring the perpetrators to justice.
May new systems of support be built to answer the needs of those who suffer.
We pray that our world can sustain its population
with food, shelter and employment.
We hold in our hearts the hope that all places will be safe to live in
and no family will be driven away from their home by violence.
We pray especially for the poor, weak, young and old
who are unable to move easily.
Wrap them in your arms of love and protection.
We ask this is the name of Jesus.
Amen.

Chapter 20

The Persecuted

He fell to the ground and heard a voice saying to him, 'Saul, Saul, why do you persecute me?'
He asked, 'Who are you, Lord?' The reply came, 'I am Jesus, whom you are persecuting.'
(Acts 9:4-5)

Reflection

Saul was persecuting Christians, imprisoning men and women of the church. He had supported the stoning of Stephen and was travelling to Damascus in order to arrest any Christians that he found in the synagogues.

The world has a long history of persecution for many reasons. Societies can find it difficult to accept difference and freedom is a precious gift that is often rare.

Prejudice is defined as preconceived opinion that is not based on reason or actual experience.

It has resulted in religious and social persecution and also apartheid based on the colour of someone's skin.

We may say that war is also persecution and that both cause oppression.

We would like to think that we have a more tolerant society today and that we uphold freedom.

Having a free press certainly helps our society to hold on to values of freedom and to halt prejudice and persecution. Disagreement still happens but we hope that people are able to

express their opinions freely.

To think about

Find out about the plight of persecuted Christians in the world today.

Prayer

Eternal Father,

We pray for all those who are victims of persecution.

May they find the freedom to live their lives without oppression.

Help us to fight any form of prejudice,

even if we find it inside ourselves.

May we think and see clearly with accepting love for humankind.

Help us to understand that your world is a place of beautiful difference

and that is a gift to all your people.

Protect those who are threatened by criminal gangs

and give strength to law enforcement to provide safety.

We pray for education and the opportunity to make good choices.

Father, we remember Saul who became Paul

as he changed to follow our Saviour.

We may not experience a road to Damascus,

but we can change if we reach out to others

showing the Saviour's love for our neighbour.

Just as the Good Samaritan helped a stranger others had turned away from,

we can value all as Jesus taught us.

Guide us as we form opinions.

Help us to be slow to judge and quick to seek understanding.

We pray for a world of freedom,

where all people are valued and respected.

We pray especially for an end to oppression, torture and the imprisonment

of those whose crime is to think differently.

We ask this in the name of your Son, our Saviour, Jesus Christ.

Amen.

Chapter 21

For Strangers

Do not neglect to show hospitality to strangers, for by doing that some have entertained angels without knowing it. (Hebrews 13:2)

Reflection

Paul advises the Hebrews to welcome strangers because God may send his angels to them.

He goes on to say that they should think of prisoners as though they themselves were in prison.

This is the same message that Jesus gave in the parable of the Good Samaritan.

Christians are told to love their neighbours and this means all people and not just those known to us.

Jesus and his disciples were made welcome as they travelled around Galilee during his ministry and they would have understood how it felt to be strangers.

In Nazareth, Jesus experienced the rejection of his own people, who failed to understand

the message he brought. Even though he was not a stranger to them, they could not accept that someone they knew could be the Messiah.

God is pleased when we show hospitality because strangers are people that we do not know yet.

Even in the time of Jesus, there would be suspicion of strangers. People travelling the road could be set upon by robbers, as the man helped by the Samaritan was. The advice to reach out to strangers could be regarded as challenging.

To think about

Is a stranger only someone we have not had the opportunity to meet before?

Prayer

Loving Father,
Help us to follow the advice of Paul
and the teaching of Lord Jesus to reach out to others.
Jesus tells us to love our neighbours
and then explains that all people are neighbours.
Guide us in our service to others.
Show us the way to help safely.
We pray for organisations that help those in need,
especially the poor and homeless.
We think of the food banks in our communities
also Crisis, Centrepoint and Shelter,
helping those without homes.
We give thanks for the work of the Salvation Army,
an army of peace and love for all,
fighting poverty and pain,
in the power of the cross.
We pray that strangers are welcomed
into our communities,
to live in peace and freedom.
Amen.

Chapter 22

For Our Differences

There is no longer Jew or Greek,
there is no longer slave or free,
there is no longer male and female;
for all of you are one in Christ Jesus.
(Galatians 3: 28)

Reflection

Paul writes to the Galatians to tell them about the Gospel of Jesus.

He explains that everyone is equal through the love of Christ, no matter who they are. This applies to the people of any nation, rich or poor. He also makes it clear that men and women are equal because they are Christians.

The love of God, brought to all through his Son Jesus Christ, takes away differences and inequalities. This is almost revolutionary, both then and even today. There have been many conflicts because people feel unable to live side by side with those who they perceive to be different. This can result in oppression and the denial of human rights as with apartheid in South Africa, the Rohingya in Myanmar (Burma) or the Uyghurs in China.

In South Africa, the black majority were ultimately successful in overturning apartheid and achieving a democratic vote for government. In this conflict, a large number of people on both sides could be said to be Christian. This makes the oppression hard to understand.

Many of the Muslim Rohingya in Myanmar were displaced to Bangladesh and some Muslim Uyghurs have escaped persecution by moving to Turkey.

Christians have been persecuted for their faith in a number of countries, including the old Soviet Union, China and states in the Middle East. The influence of the church can be seen as

a challenge to the authority of autocratic states.

To think about.

How can we celebrate our differences and develop friendship?

Prayer

Loving Father,
We give thanks for our differences.

We know that we are all special to you and we celebrate the richness of the people of your beautiful world.

Help all people to live together in peace,
able to value and respect the things they have in common and also the ways in which they differ from one another.

We pray for places in the world where there is conflict because people are not able to live side by side.

May understanding and knowledge of one with another triumph over prejudice and oppression.

We pray that human rights are maintained for all people, so that all may live in safety and security, together and at peace.

We give thanks for the United Nations, the International Court of Justice and all institutions that help us to protect the world's people.

May we support and strengthen them so that they are able to uphold justice and human rights at all times.

May all who attempt evil know

that they will be brought to justice

because we uphold the truth.

Above all, Father, we pray for peace,

so that all people can find

a place of safety for themselves

and their families.

Lord in your Mercy Hear our Prayer.

Amen.

Chapter 23

Light in our Darkness

Again Jesus spoke to them, saying,
'I am the light of the world.
Whoever follows me will never walk in darkness
but will have the light of life.'
(John 8:12)

Reflection

Jesus is speaking to the Pharisees who are questioning him trying to catch him out on religious issues.

He explains that he is the light leading us out of darkness and that anyone who follows him will walk in the light. He is the actual light in our darkness because if we do not believe in him we are in the darkness of ignorance which may lead to evil.

Jesus can guide us out of the darkness of sin into the light of redemption because he is that light.

When the world is plunged into war and conflict, it is in darkness. Sometimes Christians are caught up in the violence of dark places amid the confusion caused by sin.

True belief in Jesus helps us to find a way out of the darkness into the light of healing. This may be difficult in certain situations because we have to defend freedom and justice but we will get there because with our prayers of light, we know that our Saviour will bring us to a place of reconciliation and healing love. Perhaps sin and pain have been hiding in dark corners and they have come into the open.

If we trust in Jesus, we will find the light through our prayers and positive action.

Peace is possible and prayer shines a powerful light of peace into the darkness of fear and pain.

To think about

Imagine dark places of the world flooded with light from the cross of Jesus.

Prayer

Eternal Father,
We thank you for the gift of your Son,
who is the Light of the World.
During the Advent season especially, we wait for the light which comes anew from his birth.
We feel the special power of his light and love,
leading us forward as we hope and work for a peaceful world.
Help us to walk with him, knowing that we will have the light of life.
Guide us through the uncertainty and doubt
of a world often filled with darkness,
into the light of love and caring hopefulness.
Sometimes Father, the light seems dim and far away,
because the world is cruel.
When the Saviour comes full of light and glory,
we are restored.
May we seek him in the light of prayer,
knowing that he will lead us
to your peace.
Amen.

Chapter 24

A Future of Peace

Mark the blameless, and behold the upright,
for there is posterity for the peaceable.
(Psalm 37:37)

Reflection

This psalm of David, promises that the future is for those who choose peace.

The wicked try to kill the poor with swords and bows, but they only manage to kill themselves because their bows are broken and they use the swords on their own bodies.

This tells us that God will help good to triumph over evil in the future, so no matter how bad things are, we can hold onto our hope.

When everything seems to go wrong in the world and we feel that there is so much pain.

It can be hard to hold onto the thought that life will be better because God is on the side of good. We know it must be true and we have to try to be positive.

Another view worth thinking about, is that good can come out of bad. Even in bad situations, we find good actions and there is light at the end of a dark tunnel.

There have been so many acts of kindness over recent years as people of the world have responded to the needs of others during the global pandemic and war in Ukraine.

In this way, the future does belong to the peaceful and upright as the psalm says.

To think about

Can good come out of evil?

Prayer

Heavenly Father,
We give thanks for your word, which encourages us,
giving hope where there is little in dark times.
Help us to retain our sense of purpose and optimism,
even when everything around appears bleak and
hopeless.
We thank you for those who inspire us when we are
discouraged.
May we be uplifted and strengthened
so that we can go forward
in your name and service.
Father, we pray for a future of peace and brotherhood.
Help the peacemakers to prosper.
May the voices of reason sound loudly
above the clamour for war and disruption.
Humankind was not created to fight and destroy,
but to love and nurture.
May we fight the good fight of love,
to bring progress to all nations,
upholding the cause of justice and equality.
We pray that the future will belong to the righteous
and that it will be a future of peace.
Amen.

Chapter 25

For Communities

The second is this, 'You shall love your neighbour as yourself.'
There is no other commandment greater than these.
(Mark 12:31)

Reflection

Having been asked by one of the scribes which commandment was the first of all,

Jesus explained the two greatest commandments, to love God with all your heart and to love others as yourself.

This love of our neighbour is the cornerstone of Christianity.

In the Judgement of the Nations (Matthew 25), Jesus explains that whatever help is given to others, is given to him. Through this help, Christians attain eternal life.

Bringing peace through our communities is important for the future. Community involvement helps people to forge links with others, while building a strong system of local support. This can help mental health and prevent the formation of gangs which harm children and young people.

African Ubuntu encapsulates this idea because our humanity is linked to our recognising and understanding the humanity of others. It reflects the Christian commandment of love for our neighbour.

Caring brings with it a sense and understanding of peace. When we are able to reach out to one another, we can find our peace more easily.

The opposite would be communities fighting and arguing with each other. Local conflict can become larger and so it is important to support and build strong community links.

To think about

Do you have a strong local community?

Prayer

Loving Father,
We pray for our communities.
Help us to care for one another,
knowing that in this way we serve Jesus.
Lord, we know that people can feel isolated and lonely,
even in busy places.
Help us to develop links to support the vulnerable,
knowing that we can all experience difficult times.
As we love one another, we reach out in the name of Jesus.
Let there be no strangers in our communities,
but a welcome for friends.
In this way, we will stand up for peace and stability.
When we build towns and cities, help us to be aware of communities, so that we reduce isolation.
Help us to reach out to the young,
giving them opportunities to grow in your love.
May we build friendships and positive groups
to develop maturity and to produce true citizens.
Guide our communities towards a positive future for all people.
May we value Desmond Tutu's 'little acts of goodness that overwhelm the world'
as we seek to do your will.
In this way, we pray that we will
find our humanity through all humanity.
Amen.

Chapter 26
Teaching the Children

By contrast, the fruit of the Spirit is love, joy, peace, patience, kindness, generosity, faithfulness, gentleness, and self-control.
There is no law against such things.
(Galatians 5: 22-23)

Reflection

In his letter to the Galatians, Paul writes of the wonderful attributes that Christians gain through the influence of the Holy Spirit. These things come from Jesus Christ.

Children can be taught all these things through the word of God and this is in contrast with harmful things, such as jealousy, anger, strife, quarrels, envy and idolatry. Many of these things are the opposite of peacefulness and this suggests that if we set a good example to children, the world can grow in peace.

If we hope to have a future of peace for the world, we must teach our children that peace is the way forward and they must understand its importance for everyone.

If children are brought up to live in anger and pain, seeking vengeance and harm to others, the world will not be a peaceful place in the future.

Can we see an end to wars and conflict?

Sometimes people are not able to maintain peace and find that they have no choice but to defend themselves. This has been true of the situation in Ukraine and at other times in our history.

How do we teach children who have suffered pain and loss that they should not look for revenge and live in hate? Can we set good examples and teach them understanding and forgiveness, even when we know why they feel as they do. Despite everything, we have to believe in peace and try to teach the positive love that comes through belief in Jesus Christ and the Holy Spirit.

To think about

How do we teach children to forgive and live in peace if they have experienced war?

Prayer

Loving Father,
We thank you for the gifts of the Holy Spirit.
May we always value these attributes that we find especially as Christians.
Following Jesus, we seek to develop these fruits of the Spirit.
We try to fill our hearts to be more like our Saviour.
May we teach our children to look for these qualities in us and in themselves.
Working within your love,
we are able to show many of these gifts and yet
we know that there are so many challenges in the world
and in our daily lives.
Sometimes we have to rise above the pain that is in the world
and our children see and experience
so many things we wish they had not suffered.
Help us to show them the beauty of your creation.
We pray that they may see kindness, love, patience
and all the values that lead to peace.
Going forward in the love of Christ
we can give to them the fruits of the Holy Spirit.
In this way,
we will find true hope for the peace
of humankind.
Amen.

Chapter 27

Signs of Peace

And the dove came back to him in the evening, and there in its beak was a freshly plucked olive leaf;
so Noah knew that the waters had subsided from the earth.
(Genesis 8:11)

Reflection

Both the dove and the olive branch are the most recognisable signs of peace.

This is certainly the reason for their appearance as the logo for Sustainable Development Goal 16.

This verse from Genesis telling us about the end of the flood certainly gives great signs of peace, as Noah searched anxiously for land by sending out a dove from the ark.

God had sent the flood because people were not righteous and he wanted to start again with humankind. He had chosen Noah and his family to save the world.

After the flood, as a final promise, God created a rainbow, another sign of hope and peace. This was a covenant between himself and the people of the earth.

During the years of the pandemic, the rainbow represented a sign of hope that

life would survive this test of illness and loss. The rainbow can be seen after the darkness of the storm. It is sunshine and a fresh start.

The story of Noah reminds us of modern-day conflicts when it is necessary to rebuild for the future after so much destruction.

To think about

Can you think of other signs of peace?

Prayer

Loving Father,
Bless all peacemakers.
Be with those who seek signs of peace through the power of the Holy Spirit.
May we always be ready to offer an olive branch to those we offend,
knowing that as Christians,
the responsibility rests with us.
Father, we know it can be hard to reach out to others,
especially if we are not at peace with them.
We thank you for the example of your Son,
our Saviour Jesus Christ,
who forgave those who crucified him.
He has shown the way forward for all who follow him.
We give thanks for the sign of the dove of peace,
may it be seen as a strong commitment to healing
in all conflicts.
Father, your rainbow gives us hope
when all seems lost.
Its brightness of all colours shows that we can rebuild
our shattered towns and villages
after war.
May we grasp these signs of hope and peace
to move forward
in your love.
Amen.

Chapter 28

Peace through the Water of Life

Then the angel showed me the river of the water of life, bright as crystal, flowing from the throne of God and of the Lamb through the middle of the street of the city. On either side of the river is the tree of life with its twelve kinds of fruit, producing its fruit each month; the leaves of the tree are for the healing of the nations.
(Revelation 22: 1:2)

Reflection

We like to walk where there is water, by the sea, a river, or just near a fountain. We enjoy the sound made by running water. It gives us a calming feeling and sense of peacefulness.

When Jesus meets the Samarian woman at the well, he tells us that the water he gives brings eternal life. Jesus, the Prince of Peace, leads us to life eternal if we drink the living water. All life needs water and our bodies are up to 60% water as we inhabit a planet with a surface that is made up of around 71% water.

Jesus tells us that even though water is necessary for life on earth, he is the one who provides the spiritual water that will give us eternal life when we have left the earth.

Water is important, but the words of Jesus are more important because we will not live without them. Therefore, we can see that water is important in both a physical and spiritual sense.

In Revelation, the river of the water of life provides the leaves for the healing of nations. The prophecy tells us that the water of life flows from the throne of God and of Lord Jesus. This will bring peace to the world by paying heed to the prophecy and following God the Father, God the Son and God the Holy Spirit.

To think about

The importance of baptism with water as the symbol.
All the ways that water is important to us.

Prayer

Eternal Father,
We thank you for Jesus who is the living water,
bringing peace to the soul of the world.
Guide us as we try to follow the life that he set before us.
Help us to pray and work for peace in the world of your beautiful creation.
The Bible tells us to come to the waters if we thirst
and that thirst is satisfied through our Saviour
when he guides us to your kingdom.
Be with us as we walk beside soothing water that gives peacefulness.
Help us to recognise the calm that water brings.
May we turn to this peace to uplift our spirits
and nurture our mental health.
We pray for the sea and for the countryside.
Help us to preserve these places of calm and peace for all people.
Father, so often, I find you there.
As the waves break against the shore, or the river
flows gently touched by branches of trees in the shade.
We give thanks for the living water of Jesus,
giving peace and life eternal.
Sometimes this spiritual water wakes us to his life.
Asking the questions only he can ask.
Will we follow him?
Guide us Heavenly Father.
Amen.

Chapter 29

A Time for Peace

A time to love, and a time to hate;
a time for war, and a time for peace.
(Ecclesiastes 3: 8)

Reflection

This verse is taken from the Old Testament and can be difficult to understand in the modern age.

We would like to think that we can love rather than hate.

Even during times of acts of terror, some individuals have been able to rise above the temptation to hate. Perhaps this is because it seems to take even more away from them and to give even more pain. It can be said, I will not give the satisfaction of my hate to the perpetrator of the crime, but it does seem a very courageous feeling.

One example of this is Gordon Wilson, in regard to the death of his daughter Marie, a nurse, in an IRA bomb at a Remembrance Day parade in Enniskillen in Northern Ireland in 1987.

His words were, ' I bear no ill will. I bear no grudge.'

Gordon's call for forgiveness and reconciliation, became known as the Spirit of Enniskillen.

He went on to hold talks to end the violence of the Troubles.

Certainly if there is war, we hope that a time for peace will come.

When peace comes eventually, our prayers are still needed to make an often uneasy peace, more permanent and forgiving.

To think about

Does everything have a time? Consider the difficulty of forgiving at all times?

Prayer

Eternal Father,
We know that our world suffers war
and we understand that this may have had its time.
We pray for peace
with the passing of the time for conflict
and ask that the world may be led towards
a new time of peaceful civilisation.
May humankind retain compassion, empathy and understanding,
so that all nations can see the reason for reconciliation.
We pray for strong mediators
to lead a time for peace in our world.
May all states set aside their own interests
to work for the greater good.
Help us to value the stability
and the many benefits that peace brings,
so that we will not compromise
on this most important way forward.
May we bring education for peace
to the forefront of each nation's aims.
Father, we know that there have been times for war in the past
but we pray that the future
will be a time for peace.
Amen.

Chapter 30

Human Flourishing

As God's chosen ones, holy and beloved, clothe yourselves with compassion, kindness, humility, meekness, and patience.
(Colossians 3:12)

Reflection

Paul's letter to the church in Colossae in Phrygia, gives behavioural guidance. This is the way that God's people should behave because they are chosen by him.

If we consider the attributes mentioned, we would certainly feel that they are worthwhile

and that they would bring forward a peaceful nature so that we could be at peace with ourselves.

Human flourishing, or the ability to live a meaningful and considerate life is discussed when we think of developing our potential as human beings. This can certainly have a spiritual aspect and would include promoting peace in our attitudes towards others.

It also links with the African philosophy of Ubuntu, where we find our humanity in the humanity of others, I am because you are.

We cannot flourish as human beings if we wage war or are in conflict with our neighbours. If this occurs, we have broken the second greatest commandment given by Jesus Christ, to love our neighbours as ourselves.

Compassion is close to empathy and the ability to put ourselves in the place of others helps us to understand and flourish both as Christians and also as members of humankind.

This is important if we are to work towards a peaceful world. In our peace negotiations, we often need patience. Humility and meekness remove self-importance and drive the ability to reach out to others without feeling that this brings a loss of position. We may feel that some leaders have humility, but few would be considered to be meek. Meekness is often seen as an insult and it is not something that a world leader would promote as a positive attribute as it suggests submission.

Perhaps we must ask ourselves what Paul meant in his letter?

To think about

Is it good to be meek? Certainly, humility is a quality.

Prayer

Eternal Father,

thank you for the peace that we are able to receive

through your spirit.

We know that we must be at peace with others we meet on life's journey

if we are to flourish as human beings.

Our souls are diminished if we are in conflict with each other

yet so often, we argue and disagree.

At times, this has led to war in our world,

causing death and the destruction of cities, towns and villages.

We pray for reconciliation and lasting peace,

wherever conflict has occurred.

Guide us through prayer and the comfort of your word

to forgive and to seek forgiveness.

May we set aside the temptation to judge others.

Through compassion,

empathy and understanding,

may we seek humility in our daily lives.

Help us to be patient and kind,

even when it is difficult.

Father, we pray for the strength we need

to flourish as your holy people,

living lives to show your peace and love.

Amen.

Chapter 31

Peace in Light

But if we walk in the light as he himself is in the light,
we have fellowship with one another, and the blood of Jesus his Son cleanses
us from all sin.
(1 John 1:7)

Reflection

In his letter, John explains that God himself is light and that there is no darkness within him at all.

As Christians, we are given God's grace because Jesus was crucified. This enables us to find the peace of Christ and to come to the Father cleansed of sin, through absolution. We must turn from darkness and come to the light before we can have fellowship with

God through his Son. By confessing our sins, we are renewed in Christ.

When we think of evil, it appears to hide in the dark shadows, but if we shine the light of truth, we can deal with it in a stronger way. Freedom of speech and a free press, help to

make peace and democracy stronger. In this way, we are shining a light of truth into dark places in the world. Without the light of truth, evil acts are able to exist unchallenged.

It is hard to imagine peace without freedom and so walking in the light of peace and truth upholds civilisation.

We flourish as humankind by living in the light of truth and peace.

As people, we can find God's light through others in the light of their eyes or in a smile.

We talk of a smile that can light up a room and this is a reflection of the love of God.

This light is from within, soul light.

To think about

How can we walk more strongly in the light each day?

Prayer

Eternal Father,
We give you thanks for the light
which leads us to your peace.
The darkness of conflict
can overshadow the world we live in,
but the light of our Saviour
gives hope needed by all people.
His cross of light shines
with the power of his love.
It breaks the evil which grows slowly
as hatred.
May the light of Christ shine
into every dark corner of the world,
reaching all evil found in the hearts of men.
May the hatred of the men of war be blinded by
the light of peace.
We pray for the light of knowledge
to give understanding, compassion
and the desire for peace.
Help us to walk in the light,
showing your love to those we meet.
Amen.

Chapter 32

Places of Peace

The Holy Land

Simon answered, 'Master, we have worked all night long but have caught nothing.
Yet if you say so, I will let down the nets.'
(Luke 5:5)

Reflection

After his resurrection, Jesus met his disciples in the early morning when they had been fishing. The place is known as Mensa Christi and it is on the Sea of Galilee.

The verse from Luke, is on a plaque near the small church which has a quiet simplicity.

When I visited, I walked by the edge of the water, looking at the small stones which made up the beach.

On closer inspection, they were tiny shells, each perfectly formed.

God can make even the smallest things perfect.

There was a wooden bench with a heart in the centre and a rose at each end.

Both the rose and the heart can be said to be associated with Jesus.

It was a perfect place to sit down and look out to the calmness of the sea,

a very peaceful scene.

Galilee is a beautiful place of peace, changing but with the hazy ethereal magic

of the sea. The gentle landscape of hills, often surprisingly green, are restful and calming.

Jesus and his disciples must have felt close to this place, busy with fishermen.

Even now, Galilee is a great contrast to the busy rush of Jerusalem and still a place to find peace.

After his resurrection, Jesus sent a message to his friends that he would meet them again in Galilee. This was the place he wanted to be with them to find peace and the plans that would be made for the coming of the Holy Spirit.

Prayer

Loving Father,
We give you thanks for the beauty of Galilee,
where our Saviour walked by the shore.
The peacefulness of the water, timeless, tells of his ministry.
We are amazed by the perfection of the smallest shells
and glory in the wonder of your creation.
We reach across time and go back.
We see a figure calling to the fishermen.
Friends, have you caught anything?
Jesus gave instructions to his friends and a full net was dragged to the shore.
The Sea of Galilee still brings us closer to the time of Christ and we give thanks for this opportunity
to find the echo of Jesus and his disciples.
On calm days, we can find the peace that it brought
with the chance to speak of the kingdom of heaven.
We know that the sea can become rough with a storm suddenly changing,
and this takes us to our Lord Jesus in a boat,
calming the storm to bring peacefulness.
Help us to calm our fears and worries,
to seek the knowing that is his word, guiding us to you.
May the water deepen our faith
as we gaze into its misty stillness.
May the water, soul soothing, help us to find the peace of your kingdom with its amazing love.
Amen.

Peace Chapel and Children's Monument, North Cape

If one member suffers, all suffer together with it; if one member is honoured, all rejoice together with it.
(1 Corinthians 12:26)

Reflection

The Peace Chapel at the North Cape. St. Johannes Kappel

The chapel can be found at the northernmost point of Europe. It is inside the visitor centre, is ecumenical and popular for weddings.

There is a special sense of quiet because of the remote position. Perhaps this represents peace in a special way. The idea of being on the edge of a continent promotes deeper thought.

The altar of smooth wood with candles inside a turned over boat, creates a sense of peace with its simplicity. The lighting adds to the atmosphere, shining from spotlights onto the figure of Christ with arms outstretched as if on a crucifix on a background of stone mosaics.

Blue colour light is also used within the chapel, perhaps suggesting the sea. This contrasts with the illuminated golden rock. The chapel is perfect for the remoteness of the place, giving space for quiet meditation on the message of peace.

Outside there is a monument to the Children of the Earth, which was created in 1988.

Seven children were flown out to the North Cape to make a clay relief that was cast in bronze.

The project was to show that children of the world can work together.

The children were:

Jasmine from Tanzania, Rafael from Brazil, Ayumi from Japan, Sithedei from Thailand,

Gloria from Italy, Anton from Russia and Louise from USA.

The artist Eva Rybakken made a statue, Mother and Child, which was also displayed by the children's designs. This special place has inspired the award of a prize given annually since 1989, for a person or organisation working to improve the lives of children. Children from Mageroya Island take part in the award ceremony with a peace message.

To think about

There are many special places of holiness and peace in the world. Which ones are special to you?

Prayer

Eternal Father,
We give thanks for places
where we can come to you in prayer.
Special places of peace help us
to search into our hearts to find you,
even in the most remote and wild places on the earth.
In such places,
sometimes looking out to sea at the edge of the world,
we can feel eternity.
How small we are
and how small the actions of those on the earth
appear.
In your universe,
help us to strive for peace,
so that our children may always live and work together
in love and cooperation.
Help us to build their future
through our determination
to find a peaceful way forward
wherever there is conflict.
Lord in your mercy... Hear our prayer.
Amen.

Chapter 33

People of Peace and Justice

Whatever house you enter, first say, 'Peace to this house!'
And if anyone is there who shares in peace, your peace will rest on that person; but if not, it will return to you.
(Luke 10: 5-6)

Reflection

Jesus was telling his disciples that they would be able to give peace to others. They could do this whenever they entered a house. He was able to give them his peace on the earth and then in heaven in eternal life and they were also able to share this special gift.

In more recent times, there have been special people who have brought peace to the world in difficult times.

Mahatma Gandhi led non-violent resistance to achieve independence for India from rule by Great Britain. He campaigned to help the rights of women and to improve lives blighted by poverty. He ended untouchability which was a terrible form of discrimination. Gandhi lived in South Africa for many years and also campaigned for civil rights there. He was at an interfaith prayer meeting when he was assassinated in January 1948.

Nelson Mandela and Desmond Tutu set up the Truth and Reconciliation Commission to bring healing to the Rainbow Nation when the ANC led by Nelson Mandela defeated the inhuman system of apartheid and established the first democratically elected government of South Africa in 1994. Nelson Mandela spent 27 years as a political prisoner before his release in 1990. The Truth and Reconciliation Commission was groundbreaking in terms of making peace because it prevented further bloodshed and helped to bring information and some sense of closure for families who had lost loved ones. Taking responsibility was the first stage of a healing process for a country that had suffered a great deal.

In USA, Martin Luther King Jr. followed a non-violent campaign to achieve civil rights. Dr King spoke of his dream that black people and white people would live together in peace, yet, he was assassinated in April 1968 in Memphis, Tennessee.

Martin Luther King Jr., Desmond Tutu and Nelson Mandela were all awarded the Nobel Peace Prize. Gandhi was nominated for the prize 5 times but was never awarded it.

To think about

Who would you nominate for the Nobel Peace Prize?

Prayer

Eternal Father,
We give you thanks for all people of peace,
for leaders who have shown the world the way to forgive.
We thank you for those who have chosen non-violent methods of protest,
when it was possible.
We think of Mahatma Gandhi campaigning for racial equality in South Africa
and leading India to independence.
We thank you for the lives of Nelson Mandela, Desmond Tutu and all who
defeated the inhumanity of apartheid in South Africa.
We give thanks for reconciliation instead of retribution, when many were still bitter.
We give thanks for the dream of Martin Luther-King
and his fight for civil rights in America.
Father, may we remember these great people of peace as we go forward
in the twenty-first century.
May we hold their commitment to peace in our hearts
and vow to make their dreams and examples our hope
for a peaceful, free and united world.
Amen.

Chapter 34

Charity and Aid for Peace

If you offer your food to the hungry
and satisfy the needs of the afflicted,
then your light shall rise in
the darkness
and your gloom be like the noonday.
(Isaiah 58:10)

Reflection

This verse from Isaiah comes from a chapter about the contrast between the wicked and those who help the poor and needy. It is right to help those who are in need and to oppose injustice, thus letting the oppressed go free and helping the hungry and homeless. It is to support unselfishness and thought for others.

The passage goes on to say that the sabbath should not be used for our own selfish needs and desires, but to worship God.

The Lord will help you if you live in this way because it is the way he wishes his people to live.

When we do these things, we are like a light shining in the darkness. It is as if it is the middle of the day because there is such light. This brings us back to the light of love and goodness. As Christians, we believe that it is because of our belief in Jesus Christ, the Light of the World.

In the Letter of James to the twelve tribes, it is made clear, that as Christians, faith by itself without good works is of no use; it is dead.

To think about

How do we follow these words in our daily lives? Sunday is special, but do we find time for God and for Jesus every day?

Prayer

Loving Father,
We thank you for the example of Jesus
and the guidance of your word.
We know that our faith alone is not enough
if we are to think of ourselves as Christians.
We must care for others
and work to make the world around us a better place
because we have lived in it.
Jesus told us that what we do for others
we do for him.
May we notice where aid is needed
and offer help.
We give thanks for all those who work with charities,
making the world a safer
and more peaceful place.
We think especially of United Nations Charities,
such as UNICEF, the United Nations Children's Fund,
which gives support to all children of the world.
May all nations support the
United Nations Sustainable Development Goals,
to improve the lives of all people,
thus, helping to achieve
a peaceful world
and to deliver justice and freedom.
Amen.

Chapter 35

Peace between Faiths

With all of these, take the shield of faith,
with which you will be able to quench all the flaming arrows of the evil one.
Take the helmet of salvation, and the sword of the Spirit,
which is the word of God.
(Ephesians 6: 16-17)

Reflection

Faith may be different to many people, but it is a shield against evil.

Faith should bring peace because it stands against conflict and reaches out in reconciliation.

Christians were told by Jesus that they should forgive others many times because God forgives them. This should also be true for other faiths because God is the same living God.

Paul tells the church in Ephesus that they must proclaim the gospel of peace through the word of God.

The armour is against the devil and people of all faiths should be strong in the power of the Lord and trust in his truth.

Christianity, Judaism and Islam are Abrahamic faiths, linked to Abraham and worshipping the one God. It is helpful to think about the links between these three significant faiths, rather than the differences, in order to work for peace in the world.

Each faith has a powerful influence on followers and this can be used to bring about unrest and conflict. If faith leaders are able to use the word of God as a shield against evil, the cause of world peace would be advanced.

To think about

How can we work with those of other faiths to promote friendship and peace?

Prayer

Eternal Father,
We pray for people of all faiths who worship you.
May we join together to bring peace to the world.
Father, although we are different, we are all your children,
special in your sight.
Help us to put on your armour against the evil one.,
fighting the darkness of oppression,
wherever it is found.
May we celebrate the things we have in common,
the shield of faith, the helmet of salvation,
and the sword of the spirit,
to fight ignorance and division.
There are many people in our world,
who would spread discord between us,
yet we worship you, our Creator God.
May we find strength in your love and mercy.
As we come together to heal a world
broken in many places,
help us to bring compassion and understanding,
by reaching out in every difficult situation.
Lord in your Mercy... Hear our Prayer.
Amen.

Chapter 36

God's Covenant of Peace

I will make a covenant of peace with them;
it shall be an everlasting covenant with them;
and I will bless them and multiply them,
and will set my sanctuary among them for evermore.
(Ezekiel 37: 26)

Reflection

The prophecy of Ezekiel tells of another covenant made by God with the people of Israel, his chosen people. He promises to bless them and they will follow and obey his laws.

It is an everlasting covenant of peace.

Isaiah also speaks of an eternal covenant of peace and of the steadfast love of God, who has compassion for his people. Even if the mountains and hills disappear, the love of God is always there, even for eternal life.

God understands that humankind has disappointed him but he promises that his children will be protected from fear and terror. Weapons shall not be successful against the righteous, nor shall they be judged.

God is saying that evil cannot prosper because God's love is always there.

We can recall the psalms and think of the many ways that those who love God rejoice, give thanks and claim victory because they are sure of God's covenant.

Psalm 23 tells us that God is with us if we walk in fear and we have his goodness and mercy for ever.

To think about

God's covenant of peace is something we must work to deliver because we are all his people. Do you agree?

Prayer

Eternal Father,
We give thanks for your covenant of peace,
protecting us from our fears.
Even when evil stalks the world
and we fear for the future,
we know you are with us.
Sometimes we cannot see a way through
the struggles of hatred and oppression.
There are times we wonder what is happening,
and why?
Guide us as we seek to protect our world.
May we hold fast to your promise of peace,
to know that there is a way out of conflict.
Help us to reject war
and bring the perpetrators to justice.
Give strength to those who stand for peace and reconciliation.
May they heal the wounds of bloodshed and division,
slowly building a lasting and healing peace,
enfolded within your love.
Amen.

Conclusion

And let the peace of Christ rule in your hearts,
to which indeed you were called in the one body.
And be thankful.
(Colossians 3:15)

Paul's letter to the Colossians tells of the new life in Christ.

His advice to them is to rid themselves of anger and disagreement. He tells them to forgive each other and to show compassion, kindness and patience, along with other qualities.

Paul's message is that the peace of Christ should rule the hearts of all Christians and this will result in peace among them. It is a message for the whole world. Love for God and love for each other, is central to the teaching of Jesus Christ as the two greatest commandments. If we follow the rules, we will find the peace of Christ and live in peace with the world.

Prayer is powerful and we believe that like faith, it can move mountains.

Our prayers for peace are among the most important prayers we can offer to God the Father because we have seen the suffering that war brings.

Perhaps we thought that we had left conflict behind to a large extent in our modern, civilised world. Sadly, we still find that humankind can fall below any low level of behaviour we can imagine.

The war in Ukraine, has reminded us, as other conflicts have, that man is capable of inhuman behaviour. Even at these times, we see great acts of kindness and love shown towards those who are suffering, yet this does not take away the pain and horror of the situation.

Our prayers for peace are for the cessation of conflict, for healing and reconciliation, rather than retribution and then for successful rebuilding and restoration.

Forgiveness can be so difficult after the horror of war and the seeds of future conflict lie dormant, even for many years.

In prayers for peace, we must pray for forgiveness, healing and reconstruction, not only of buildings and infrastructure, but of people's hearts and minds.

These things are difficult, but possible within the love and example of our Saviour, Jesus Christ. This must be the conclusion of every prayer for peace, that in his love and light, we will find a way forward towards a peaceful world.

In the name of Christ, Amen.

Charities

Please pray for all charities working to promote peace in the world. Some are mentioned below:

ChildAid to Eastern Europe

ChildAid to Eastern Europe is a Christian organisation, started in 1973 to support Christians in the former Soviet Union. With the end of communism, it continued to work to provide aid to families, children and young people to give the disadvantaged and vulnerable, hope and opportunity.

Working with partners , ChildAid supports both short- and long-term programmes to help families, orphans, disabled children and young people.

The work of the charity has become increasingly important during the recent war and crisis in Ukraine and the surrounding areas. The support given has changed in order to meet emergency needs as well as continuing the usual projects where possible.

The 50th anniversary of ChildAid in 2023 will be difficult to celebrate, even though so much has been achieved. There will be a continuing need to help Ukraine with reconstruction, even when the peace we hope for is a reality.

The families receiving help from ChildAid are especially vulnerable at this time. The project partners have adapted the support they provide, including offering a bomb shelter and gathering children together for summer camps as they usually do.

In Moldova, ChildAid is helping to support refugees, especially in the specialised Tony Hawks Centre for children and young people with special needs, providing therapy and rehabilitation programmes as well as food, hygiene products and clothes.

In addition to financial support, prayer meetings have taken place to pray for peace and help at this very difficult time.

For further and up to date information, please visit the website.

Website: www.childaidee.org.uk

ChildAid, PO Box 200, Bromley, BR1 1QF

Mosaic Middle East

The charity brings hope and healing to the Middle East, working with vulnerable and persecuted minorities. They are motivated by Christian compassion.

Their work includes: funding the medical clinic at St. Georges, Baghdad, jobs through sustainable enterprise and economic development (Nineveh Seed), community centres (Olive Tree Centres) to help Iraqi Christian refugees, peace building across all faiths and emergency relief (for example winter coats to Yazidi teenage girls in their refugee camp).

Mosaic Middle East believes in the power and importance of prayer.

Website: www.mosaicmiddleeast.org

Help The Persecuted

This charity helps persecuted Christian believers with field ministry teams, working with church partners in local areas. Their aim is to build long term discipleship relationships so that the church can flourish, even in hostile regions.

They provide practical support, including safe houses and evacuation where necessary.

Recently, they have helped people who have been persecuted in Afghanistan, by helping to resettle people to areas where they can rebuild their lives. Support includes coordinating paperwork, providing housing, expenses and food supplies.

The aim of the charity is to Rescue, Restore and Rebuild.

It is possible to become a prayer partner to help this charity.

Website: www.htp.org

Release International

Release International was founded in 1968, as a Christian ministry working through local church partners in around 30 countries of the world. It is inspired by the ministry of Pastor Richard Wurmbrand to love and serve persecuted Christians.

The ministry is based on Hebrews 13 v3:

Remember those who are in prison,
as though you were in prison with them;
those who are being tortured,
as though you yourselves were being tortured.

Recently, I attended a church lunch and talk when Rev. Robert de Berry and his team of cyclists completed an amazing cycle ride to raise funds for Release in May and June 2022.

We commemorate the Day of the Christian Martyr on 29th June. On this day, we remember the 4,000 Christians killed for their faith every year.

Website: www.releaseinternational.org

In 1981, a United Nations resolution established International Day of Peace (World Peace Day) which is observed each year on 21st September.

International Day of Friendship is on 30th July. The UN General Assembly introduced International Day of Friendship in 2011. This recognised that if friendship and understanding are encouraged, countries are more likely to be at peace.

All the darkness in the world cannot extinguish the light of a single candle.
- St. Francis of Assisi.

As we light our candles and offer our prayers for peace, we can hold this powerful message in our hearts.